Little Dorrit
A Brief Introduction

Also by Donald S. Hair

From Rock's Mills Press
Souwesto Lives: John Hair and Alice Runnalls (2017)
A Professor's Life (2022)

From Other Publishers
Fresh Strange Music: Elizabeth Barrett Browning's Language (2015)
The Dramatic Imagination of Robert Browning: A Literary Life
(co-authored with Richard S. Kennedy) (2007)
Robert Browning's Language (1999)
Tennyson's Language (1991)
Domestic and Heroic in Tennyson's Poetry (1981)
Browning's Experiments with Genre (1972)

Little Dorrit
A Brief Introduction

Donald S. Hair

Rock's Mills Press
Rock's Mills, Ontario • Oakville, Ontario
2023

Published by
Rock's Mills Press
www.rocksmillspress.com

Copyright © 2023 by Donald S. Hair.
All rights reserved. No part of this publication may be reproduced, distributed, or transmitted in any form or by any means, including photocopying, recording, or other electronic or mechanical methods, without the prior written permission of the publisher.

For information, contact the publisher at customer.service@rocksmillspress.com.

Little Dorrit is a big book, and though its eight hundred pages are not more than some of the long novels popular in our own day—the last in the *Harry Potter* series, for instance—still its bulk is daunting. For someone coming to the novel for the first time, there are one or two things to be kept in mind.

First, Dickens is not a subtle writer. One has only to look at the repetitions in the first chapter, where the "prison taint" is on everything, or at the chapter on the Circumlocution Office, where "how not to do it" is the watchword of government, to know that one could not possibly miss the point Dickens is making. Secondly, for all his lack of subtlety, Dickens is wide-ranging, complex, and suggestive. That is because of his much celebrated "inventiveness," not just of character and situation but of the concrete detail, what George Orwell calls (in one of the best essays written on Dickens's fiction) the apparently "unnecessary detail" that does not advance the story in any way and yet is absolutely essential in creating (what Orwell calls) "the special Dickens atmosphere." Mrs. Merdle's parrot, for instance (I. xx). It adds nothing to the story, but it does bite, and it is always turning itself upside down. So why is it there? As one proceeds to read about the multiple characters, their relations and opinions and treatment of each other, one begins to sense that the world Dickens is creating in the novel is a world that, like the parrot, has inverted or reversed itself and is in need of being set right. All those "unnecessary details" are not only effective in establishing a vividly realized "atmosphere" but affective as

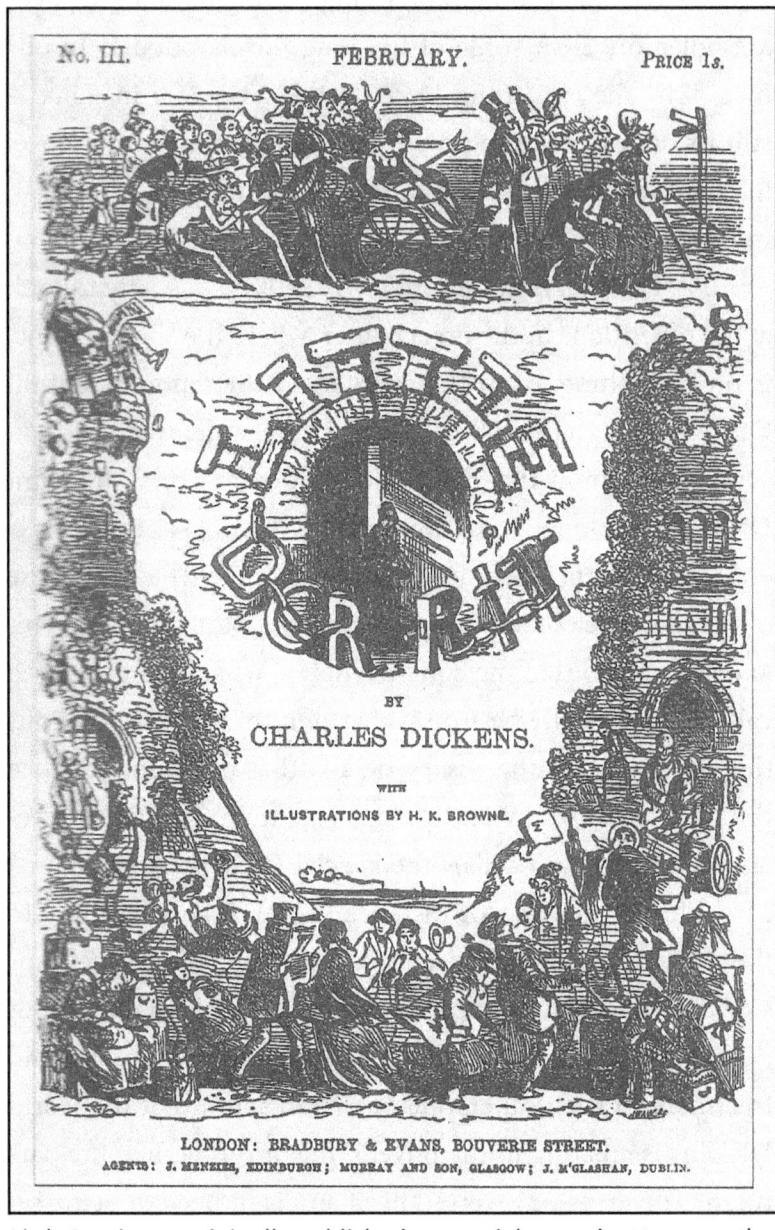

Little Dorrit was originally published as a serial over nineteen months. Above, H.K. Browne's design and illustration for the monthly parts. This installment was first published in February 1856.

well: they appeal to the feelings and emotions that underpin our intellectual response to the story.

That appeal is crucial to Dickens's purpose. For *Little Dorrit* is a novel of social and political protest, where Dickens is exposing and attacking that most difficult of social ills to define precisely, the one that people sometimes refer to as the "system." People still blame disappointments and failures on the "system" as a way of escaping personal responsibility for any setbacks, which are then "nobody's fault." "Nobody's fault" was Dickens's original title for the novel, and it is of course ironic: something that is "nobody's fault" is everybody's fault.

There were plenty of faults to find at the time between 1855 and 1857 when Dickens was writing the novel and issuing it in monthly parts: there were the revelations of the mismanagement and bad judgment in the conduct of the Crimean War (revelations focused in Tennyson's famous line, "Some one had blundered"); there was the investigation into the incompetence of government departments, filled with people who had gained their posts through the status conferred on them by birth or wealth but who had no talent for administration and no motive in undertaking it other than self-interest; there were the failures of promoters and speculators like George Hudson, the "railway king," whose schemes collapsed in the late 1840s, and John Sadleir, a Member of Parliament, banker and forger, who poisoned himself on Hampstead Heath in 1856. "I shaped Mr. Merdle himself out of that precious rascality," Dickens tells a correspondent (*Letters* 8. 79).

Current as *Little Dorrit* was, Dickens does a curious thing for a novelist with his agenda. One would expect him to set

This engraving appeared in *Harper's New Monthly Magazine* (volume 12, number 69) in February 1856.

the story in the era in which he was writing, but instead he locates the action thirty years earlier, about 1825. Moreover, by the time he was writing many of those specific ills had been addressed. Imprisonment for debt, for instance. The Marshalsea prison figures in a large way in the story, but in fact imprisonment for small debts had been abolished in 1844, and the Marshalsea itself had been torn down (in his preface Dickens recounts a personal visit to the parts that remained standing). Administrative reform was in progress in the 1850s, and the handling of patents, which so frustrates the engineeer and inventor Daniel Doyce in the novel, had

Artist Fredrick Bernard's rendering of Dickens as a boy working in a factory to help support his family, during the period when his father had been sent to the Marshalsea Prison.

been improved with the Patent Reform Act of 1852. Yet all these things Dickens attacks as if nothing had been done about them.

We begin to realize that Dickens's real object is to expose recurring elements in human nature that are the sources of incompetence, inertia, and rigidity: certain attitudes, prejudices, motives. The self-interest of the Barnacles (who attach themselves to the ship of state in the Circumlocution Office) is obvious enough, but Dickens extends that laying open of responsibility to all classes in society, and even to characters who are otherwise admirable or comic. To Mr. Meagles, for instance, who is middle class. He describes himself as "practical," but his attitude to Daniel Doyce—"no inventor can be a man of business, you know"—causes Arthur Clennam to wonder "whether there might be in the breast of this honest, affectionate, and cordial Mr. Meagles, any microscopic portion of the mustard-seed that had sprung up into the great tree of the Circumlocution Office" (I. xvi). Or the working-class Mrs. Plornish, a comic character who sets herself up as a translator for the Italian immigrant Cavaletto. She is celebrated for saying to the injured Cavaletto "Me ope you leg well soon," considered by her neighbours as "but a very short remove indeed from speaking Italian," and she takes (what the narrator generously calls) "pardonable pride" in her incompetence (I. xxv).

With such an agenda, we would expect Dickens to choose the form of fiction apparently best suited to showing ills as they actually are: that is, realism. Realism and romance were the binary literary critics and reviewers used to describe the two main kinds of fiction of the mid-Victorian period, and while Thackeray was the great champion of realism, Dickens championed romance and its appeal to the imagination. For while realism portrays events as probable and people as complex, romance presents them not as they actually are but as they appear to us, in the light of our hopes and fears, our wishes and aversions and nightmares. Romance has an important bearing on Dickens's shaping of his plot.

At the heart of *Little Dorrit* is a mystery, as there often is in a Dickens novel (think of *Great Expectations*, for instance, or *Bleak House*), and Dickens introduces it with his hero Arthur Clennam's return to his mother's house, his first sight of Little Dorrit, and his suspicion that his family's business has in some way or other been the cause of injury to and ruin of others, and that he ought to make reparation. His resolve gradually focuses on Little Dorrit herself. The mystery has some conventional romance elements—twin brothers, an iron box that goes missing, revelatory letters, a scheming manservant, and a blackmailer—and while I am not about to spoil the revelation for the reader, I do want to draw attention to the fact that the solution to the mystery turns upon concerns that were central to Dickens's thinking as a novelist. He was always promoting the imagination as a healing alternative in a commercial society devoted to facts and to "being practical"—think of *Hard Times*—and the editorial policy of *Household Words*, the periodical of which Dickens was editor, was "To show to all, that in all familiar things, even in those which are repellant on the surface, there is Romance enough, if we will find it out." Dickens was always pressing his managing editor on that policy, even on one occasion resorting to an upper-case imperative: "KEEP 'HOUSEHOLD WORDS' IMAGINATIVE!" (*Letters* 7. 200).

Arthur Clennam embodies his creator's concerns. "I am the only child of parents who weighed, measured, and priced everything," Arthur says, of parents who practised "a stern religion" (I.ii), and who were inexorably opposed to "those accursed snares which are called the Arts" (II.xxx). Yet nature was his foster mother, leading him to dwell "on hopeful promises, on playful fancies, on the harvests of tenderness and humility that lie hidden in the early-fostered seeds of the imagination" (II.xxxiv).

One conventional wish-fulfilment plot is the rags-to-riches story, and Dickens uses that as the main framework of this novel: the title of the first book is "POVERTY," and of the second "RICHES." Both have a literal as well as a metaphorical meaning. Within that larger design Dickens sets another conventional plot of romance, the education of the hero. Usually that education is a conversion like that of Scrooge in *A Christmas Carol*, but Arthur's education is of a different sort. From the beginning he is good-hearted, but he lacks the will to bring his good nature to bear on society. "I have no will" (I.ii), he says when we first meet him, and that want is especially evident in the chapters where he fails to act upon his feelings of love for Minnie ("Pet") Meagles. His education

Portrait of Charles Dickens around the time that *Little Dorrit* was published by the Belgian artist and lithographer Charles Baugniet.

takes the form of learning how to live in an imperfect world: at the end of the story, he and Little Dorrit go "down into a modest life of usefulness and happiness" (II.xxxiv). They have not changed the world, but they have taken control over their part of it, and so become Dickens's model for the reform he is promoting.

The title page from the first book publication of *Little Dorrit* (Bradbury and Evans, 1857). The illustration is by Hablot Knight Browne, who also illustrated the serial edition of the novel, and shows Amy leaving the Marshalsea Prison.

Dickens creates much of the "atmosphere" of his novels through the speeches of his characters. There is an astonishing range of speech patterns in *Little Dorrit*, so much so that it held a special interest for Mikhail Bakhtin, the great Russian critic and theorist of the novel and of *heteroglossia*, its multiplicity of voices. Such diversity serves Dickens's purposes in wonderfully effective ways: images like the upside-down parrot are not the only evidence of a world in reverse. For instance, in response to Clennam's inquiries about her son's growing up with Little Dorrit, Mrs. Chivery answers with sentences that go forward and then run backwards: "He played with her as a child when in that yard a child she played" (I. xxii). Or Mr. Casby's instructions to his money-grubber Pancks, who collects rents from the inhabitants of Bleeding Heart Yard: "You are paid to squeeze, and you must squeeze to pay"—an unexpectedly "brilliant turn" in which Casby takes "great satisfaction" (II. xxxii). Then there is the speech of Clennam's first love, Flora Finching, whose mind is imprisoned in a web of associations, every one of which she voices in a torrent of syntax, "pointing her conversation with nothing but commas, and very few of them" (I. xiii); and the contrasting speech of her constant companion, Mr. F.'s Aunt, whose one-sentence pronouncements apparently have no connection with anything. But this contrast too serves Dickens's purposes. In romance, single characters often split in two—this is the Doppelganger, best known in Stevenson's Dr. Jekyll and Mr. Hyde—and while Flora is the sentimental and nostalgic half of the character, Mr. F.'s Aunt,

This photograph of the Marshalsea Prison was taken around 1897. The prison closed in 1842 and the buildings were sold, to be rented out for shops and rooms. Today only the brick wall that was the prison's southern wall remains.

who takes a particular dislike to Clennam, manifests all the spite and fury of the disappointed and abandoned woman. Then there is the speech of Lord Decimus Barnacle, "elephantine trots … through a jungle of overgrown sentences" (II. xxiv); and of Barnacle Junior, who has a verbal tic not unknown in our own day—"you know"—while he is complaining about Clennam's upsetting the Circumlocution Office by insisting on knowing the facts of the Dorrit case. Barnacle Junior's "You know" plays off ironically against Clennam's "I want to know" (I. x), in the verbal standoff the Circumlocution Office is so adept at creating.

A note on Dickens himself. The reader would do well to keep separate Dickens the man and Dickens the novelist. "My father was not a good man," Dickens's daughter Kate did not hesitate to say many years after her father's death. She was referring to his treatment of her mother and to his taking a mistress, the actress Ellen Ternan. (Among other things, Dickens had a partition built in the bedroom he had until then shared with his wife Catherine.) Claire Tomalin's 2011 biography tells the whole sad story.

The authoritative edition of *Little Dorrit* is the Clarendon issued by Oxford University Press in 1979. It includes the "number plans," Dickens's working notes for the whole novel. John Butt and Kathleen Tillotson prove just how useful those notes can be in their 1957 study, *Dickens at Work*. On romance in Victorian fiction, see Edwin Eigner's 1978 *The Metaphysical Novel in England and America* and Donald Stone's 1980 *The Romantic Impulse in Victorian Fiction*.

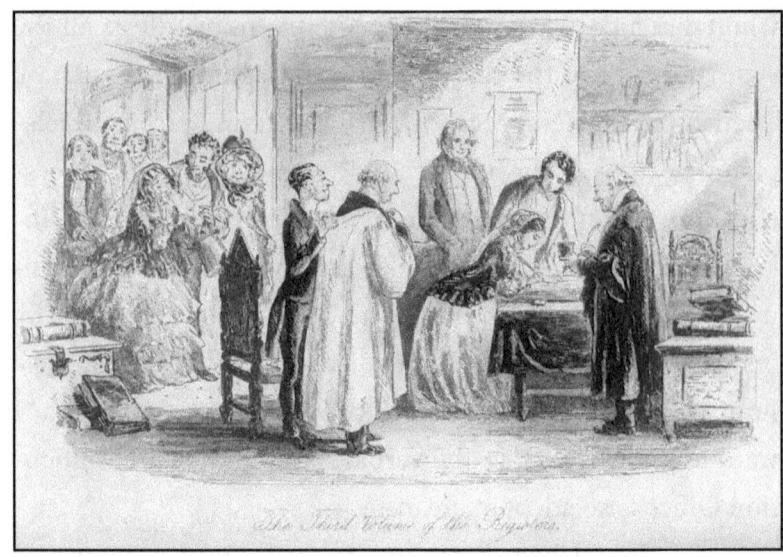

Little Dorrit ends with the marriage of Arthur Clennam and Little Dorrit. The novel's last paragraphs are as memorable in their own way as the opening lines of *A Tale of Two Cities*:

> They all gave place when the signing [of the marriage registry] was done, and Little Dorrit and her husband walked out of the church alone. They paused for a moment on the steps of the portico, looking at the fresh perspective of the street in the autumn morning sun's bright rays, and then went down.
>
> Went down into a modest life of usefulness and happiness. Went down to give a mother's care, in the fulness of time, to Fanny's neglected children no less than to their own, and to leave that lady going into Society for ever and a day. Went down to give a tender nurse and friend to Tip for some few years, who was never vexed by the great exactions he made of her in return for the riches he might have given her if he had ever had them, and who lovingly closed his eyes upon the Marshalsea and all its blighted fruits. They went quietly down into the roaring streets, inseparable and blessed; and as they passed along in sunshine and shade, the noisy and the eager, and the arrogant and the froward and the vain, fretted and chafed, and made their usual uproar.

Critical studies of Dickens and of *Little Dorrit* specifically are far too many to be listed here, but there are exhaustive chapter-by-chapter notes and a lengthy bibliography in Trey Philpotts' 2003 *Companion to* Little Dorrit.

About the Author

Donald S. Hair is professor emeritus in the Department of English and Writing Studies at Western University in London, Ont. A specialist in Victorian literature, he is the author of a number of other books, including *Browning's Experiments with Genre*, *Robert Browning's Language*, *Domestic and Heroic in Tennyson's Poetry*, *Tennyson's Language*, *The Dramatic Imagination of Robert Browning: A Literary Life* (with Richard S. Kennedy), and *Fresh Strange Music: Elizabeth Barrett Browning's Language*. Dr. Hair's *Souwesto Lives*—a social history of his family and the region of southwestern Ontario in which they settled—and his memoir *A Professor's Life* are both published by Rock's Mills Press. He was the recipient of the Edward G. Pleva Award for Excellence in Teaching in 2001–02 as well as the OCUFA Teaching and Academic Librarianship Award in 1991.

Fanny and Little Dorrit call on Mrs. Merdle. Illustration by Hablot Knight Browne, who was also known by his pen name "Phiz."

Historical plaque at the location of the Marshalsea Prison along Dickens Walk in Southwark, London. *(Photo courtesy trailerfullofpix via Flickr.)*

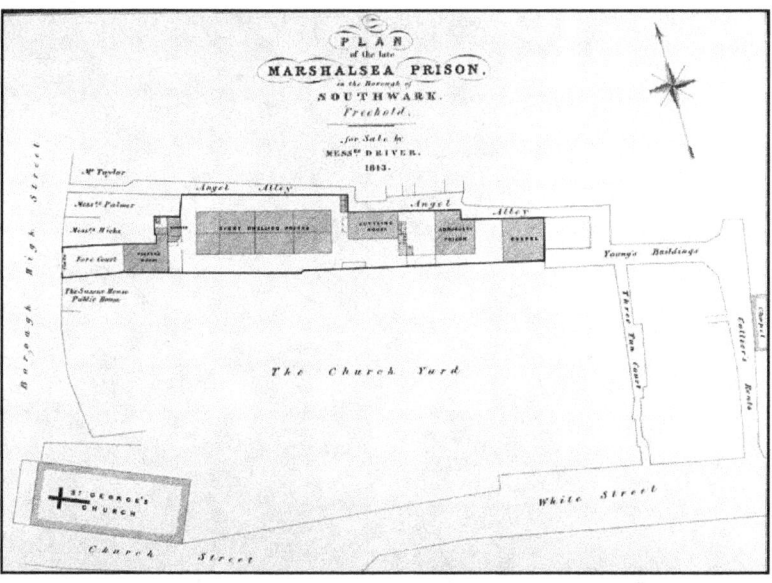

Plan of the second Marshalsea Prison, drawn up in 1843 after it was closed. *(Courtesy British Library via Wikimedia Commons.)*

www.ingramcontent.com/pod-product-compliance
Lightning Source LLC
Chambersburg PA
CBHW070120110526
44587CB00016BA/2743